Paleo Pressure Cooker Recipes:

101 Pressure Cooker Recipes For Quick & Easy, One Pot, Paleo Meals

By

Ashley Peters

As a "Thank You" for purchasing this book, I want to give you a gift absolutely 100% Free

** Follow the instructions at the end of this book to receive Healthy Pressure Cooker Recipes FREE **

Table of Contents

Introduction

Congratulations and Thank You!

I want to start by thanking you for downloading the book, "Paleo Pressure Cooker Recipes: 101 Pressure Cooker Recipes For Quick & Easy, One Pot, Paleo Meals" I am honored to be helping you on this journey to create quick & easy Pressure Cooker Recipes!

One of the advantages of following a specific diet nowadays is that there are so many resources available to you to really expand your palate, instead of opting to sacrifice tastes and quality in the name of following a regimen. For this reason, the pressure cooker is one of the most vital tools that you can add to your culinary repertoire, as it provides for versatility in your recipes and can help you to prepare some of the healthiest meals you have ever tasted.

The pressure cooker was designed to speed the cook time of foods, and its usage actually dates back to the late 1700s. Current pressure cookers look like little pots with a thick handle and a latch that secures the top of the pot in place. In order to activate the speedy cook time, all you have to do is place your ingredients into the pot, add a bit of water, and boil all of the ingredients together. The pressure inside the vessel - hence the name - will build up significantly, causing all of your meats, vegetables, and grains within the body of the pot to cook quickly and evenly. This method has effectively cut cook time of certain recipes virtually in half, which is why it has become such a popular item in kitchens around the world.

The best part about pressure cookers, however, is how compatible they are with various diets. The Paleo diet, in particular, is one that you can continue with ease when you purchase and start to utilize a pressure cooker, as the modes of preparation will allow you to remain faithful to the guidelines. No matter what type of Paleo recipe you are trying to whip up, the pressure cooker is the tool that you should turn to if you want to prepare healthy meals in half the time. One of the benefits of using this piece of equipment is that it yields a much healthier dish, seeing as there is no frying involved to get that rich seared and steamed taste.

Throughout Paleo Pressure Cooker Recipes, you will find a plethora of dishes that you can prepare using your pressure cooker to make delicious Paleo meals for yourself and for your loved ones. They will appreciate not only the taste, but the high nutrient value that is packed in everything you make!

Thanks again for downloading this book, I Hope You Enjoy It

What is Pressure Cooking?

Of all the cooking fads that have emerged in recent years, pressure cooking continues to be one of the easiest, quickest, and most effective methods. This type of cooking has been around for generations, and has maintained its popularity in kitchens across the world. Essentially, pressure cooking relies on what its name entails: pressure. It is a culinary process that was invented by Denis Papin, a Frenchman who sought to combine what he knew about the science of pressure and cooking. He thought that combining steam pressure from his heavy lidded pot could reduce the amount of time it took him to cook something. After years of trying to make the pot and valve combo safe for use, pressure cooking was introduced to the world. From start to finish, pressure cooking is a simple way to prepare food in a delicious and easy method.

To start the process, a small pot with a seal is filled with either water or broth to flavor the dish. Real pressure cookers have a valve-type handle on the top, which allows the steam either to stay in the pot or escape depending on the position of the valve. It is important that the valve be placed in the closed position when the cooking begins. Before closing the lid, food is put in the pot with the water or the broth, and then it is sealed tight. When the liquid is brought to a boil, an intense amount of steam is created, and therefore causes a buildup of pressure. The food on the inside cooks quickly, since the time that it normally takes the liquid to boil is actually cut in half thanks to the steam pressure.

Pressure cooking is different from steam cooking, however, due to the fact that steaming does not offer the high-intensity pressure that is created only when the pot is sealed air-tight and the steam from the liquid is allowed to rise, but to not escape. One surprising result of pressure cooking is that the food can actually caramelize and take on the appearance of having been seared, which gives a profound flavor to the ingredients that are being prepared.

Pressure Cooker Benefits

One method of cooking that has always provided inherent benefits is pressure cooking. Designed centuries ago to combine steam pressure and cooking, this mode of preparation cuts average cooking time in half. It relies on the steam pressure created from sealing boiling water in a pot with its contents, cooking all of the ingredients on the inside. A fundamental benefit to pressure cooking is the time it saves from start to finish. Due to the fact that the temperature inside the pot is so high, the food cooks in nearly half the time, yet does not sacrifice any taste or flavor. Not only does it save people time, pressure cooking also saves them money. With the decreased use of the stove, people have reported a dip in their energy bills thanks to this quick one-pot cooking method.

The flavor of food is also exquisitely preserved in pressure cooking. While cooking food in a conventional way can have the flavor either evaporate with the steam or remain in bits at the bottom of a pan, the flavor of pressure cooked food stays within the pot at all times. This delivers a robust burst of flavor that otherwise would have been lost. One rule of thumb to preserving the scrumptious tastes of meat, for example, is to cook it in oil, remove to a plate, and then pressure cook it again with broth to conserve all of the flavors.

Pressure cooked meals are also extremely healthy, seeing as water and steam heat is really all that is needed to cook the food through and through. No fattening oils and deep-frying are needed to create well-rounded family favorites. Vegetables and other vitamin-rich foods also maintain their highest level of nutritional value. The longer vegetables cook, the more nutrients they lose; therefore the pressure cooker allows them to stay as vitamin-packed as possible. The cleanup is another attraction to the pressure cooker; since the meals are normally prepared only in the cooker, there is just one pot left to clean when dinner is through.

Pressure Cooker Tips

Since their invention in the 1600s by a Frenchman, pressure cookers have been known for around the world to prepare quick, healthy meals that rely on steam pressure to cook, caramelize, and sear various types of foods. Yet in using the pressure cooker there are different tricks that you can tuck into your pocket to help you make the most of your pressure cooking experience.

The first rule of thumb is not to add too much liquid to the pot. When normally boiling liquid, the pot is kept open or a light lid is placed on top with the expectation that some of the water will evaporate. This is not so for the pressure cooker: because the lid is sealed shut, no water can evaporate out of the pot. It is therefore recommended that you use less liquid than you would when you usually cook. That said, if too much water is added to the pot and you have already put the food in, you can simply decrease the amount of liquid by boiling it without the lid on.

The process of pressure cooking should always begin with very high heat. Then, when the liquid boils, the heat is turned down to a low level. That way, the pressure is regulated and maintained while the food continues to cook, and will not exceed unsafe levels on the inside.

Timing is also an essential component to pressure cooking. When following directions, it is recommended to time the cooking according to the exact instructions on the package and not much longer. Overcooking food can happen quite easily with this method, so it is crucial to be as accurate as possible. The harder and more dense the food, the longer it will take to cook.

Finally, an important rule when it comes to pressure cooking is the size of the food. If your recipe calls for ingredients that are chopped or cubed, be sure that all of the pieces are roughly the same size. This ensures that all of the food is cooked to the same degree of completion, and that nothing comes out either under- or overcooked. And with all

Paleo Pressure Cooker Chinese Breakfast Tea Eggs

INGREDIENTS:

3 Eggs, Hard-boiled and cooled
¼ cup coconut aminos
1 Lemon, zested
2 teabags, Earl Gray Black Tea
1 Tbsp. Cloves (the spice)
1 Tbsp. Black Pepper Corns
1 Tbsp. Juniper Berries
2 Bay Laurel Leaves

INSTRUCTIONS:

•Crack the eggs and discard the shells.
•Add all the ingredients with a cup of water in a heatproof container except the coconut aminos.
•Bring to boil and then add the eggs and coconut aminos with some extra water to cover.
•Using a tin foil, cover it.
•Add a cup of water to the pressure cooker and place the steamer basket in it.
•Lower the container into the pressure cooker.
•Cover the pressure cooker and set to low pressure.
•Increase the heat until it reaches pressure and then reduce the heat.
•Cook for 20 minutes.
•Once the cooking time is complete, turn off the flame.
•Release the pressure using the natural release method.
•Uncover and leave to cool.
•Remove the eggs.

Paleo Pressure Cooker Breakfast Poached Eggs in Bell Peppers

INGREDIENTS:

2 slices of Paleo bread, toasted
2 slices of Paleo Cheddar cheese
1 small bunch of Rucola
2 Fresh Eggs, refrigerated
2 Bell Peppers, ends cut off
Hollandaise sauce:
⅔cup Paleo mayonnaise
1½ tsp. Dijon mustard
3 tbsp. orange juice
1 tsp. fresh lemon juice
1 tbsp. white wine vinegar
½ tsp. salt
1 tsp. of Turmeric

INSTRUCTIONS:

•Whisk together all the ingredients of the Hollandaise sauce until smooth.
•Add a cup of water and place the steamer basket in the pressure cooker.
•Chop the top ends of the bell pepper and scoop out the seeds and membranes to make cups.
•Break the eggs into the cups and cover with a tin foil.
•Place the bell peppers in the steamer basket.
•Cover the pressure cooker and set to low pressure.
•When it reaches pressure cook for 3-4 minutes.
•Once the cooking time is complete, turn off the flame.
•Release the pressure using the natural release method.
•Stack the toast, cheese, rucola and pepper cups with a spoon of Hollandaise sauce.

Paleo Pressure Cooker Breakfast Burrito
(Servings: 4)

INGREDIENTS:

    2 tbsp. of olive oil
    8 boiled eggs, peeled and diced
    1/4 cup red onion, diced
    1/2 cup tomato, diced
    1/4 cup cilantro, chopped
    1/4 cup water
    1 tsp. of salt
    4 large Paleo tortillas, steamed
    1 avocado, peeled and sliced

INSTRUCTIONS:

•Heat olive oil in a pressure cooker over medium flame and then add the eggs and stir well.
•Sauté for a few minutes and then add the tomato, onion, cilantro, salt and water.
•Close the pressure cooker and bring to high pressure.
•Cook for 6 minutes and then remove from the heat.
•Release the pressure using the quick release method.
•To prepare the burrito, place a tortilla first and place one-fourth of the egg mixture and one fourth of the avocado slices at the middle of the tortilla.
•Roll the burrito.
•Repeat for all burritos.

Paleo Pressure Cooker Mushroom & Spinach Breakfast Frittata

INGREDIENTS:

    1/2 cup frozen spinach, thawed, drained and squeezed dry
    1/2 cup fresh button mushrooms, cleaned and sliced
    2 green onions, chopped
    4 large eggs, beaten
    1/2 tsp. ground oregano
    1/2 tsp. ground thyme
    Pinch salt and pepper
    1/4 cup Paleo Cheddar cheese, grated

INSTRUCTIONS:

• Coat the inner pot of the cooker with a cooking spray.
• Combine the spinach, onions and mushrooms in a bowl.
• Mix in the oregano, eggs, salt, pepper, thyme and cheese.
• Spoon the batter into the inner pot and close the cooker.
• Press the white rice button on the cooker and cook for 12 minutes.
• The eggs should be firm on the bottom and set on the top, once ready.
• Slice the frittata into wedges.

Paleo Pressure Cooker Zuchinni Breakfast Frittata
INGREDIENTS:

4 oz. bacon, chopped
1 zucchini, sliced thin
4 oz. fresh mushrooms, sliced thin
Pinch each of basil, salt, and pepper
4 eggs
1 tbsp. water

INSTRUCTIONS:

• Fry the bacon until crispy in an uncovered pressure cooker.
• Reserve only 1 tbsp. of fat and add the veggies and cook till soft.
• Spread the veggies in an even layer on the bottom of the cooker.
• Whisk the rest of the ingredients together in a bowl and pour it over the veggies.
• Cover the pressure cooker and heat to pressure.
• Release the pressure using the natural release method.

Paleo Pressure Cooker Breakfast Devilled Eggs

INGREDIENTS:

2 cups water, or as needed
8 fresh eggs

INSTRUCTIONS:

•Fill the pressure cooker with the minimum amount of water.
•Place the steamer basket in the pressure cooker and place the eggs in it.
•Cover the pressure cooker and bring to low pressure.
•Cook for 6 minutes and then allow the pressure to drop.
•Release the pressure using the quick release method and then transfer the eggs into a bowl of ice cold water.
•Cool completely.

Paleo Pressure Cooker Breakfast Casserole

INGREDIENTS:

4-5 cups frozen shredded sweet potatoes
½ cup cooked bacon broken up
6 eggs
½ cup coconut milk
6 tbsp. water
2 tbsp. olive oil
Paleo Cheddar cheese for garnish

INSTRUCTIONS:

•Heat olive oil in a cooker and toss in the shredded sweet potatoes.
•Sprinkle the bacon on top.
•Beat the eggs, coconut milk and water and pour it over the bacon in the cooker.
•Press the cook button and when the cooker pops up, add 3 tbsp. water and press the cook button again.
•Sprinkle the cheese on top and leave to melt.

Paleo Pressure Cooker Breakfast Hash

INGREDIENTS:

6 eggs, beaten
1 cup shredded Paleo Cheddar cheese
1 cup chopped breakfast ham, shredded
6 small sweet potatoes, shredded
¼ cup water
2 tbsp. olive oil

INSTRUCTIONS:

•Heat olive oil in a cooker.
•Squeeze the shredded potatoes to remove the moisture out.
•Brown the shredded potatoes in the heated oil.
•Add the water and the remaining ingredients and mix.
•Cover the pressure cooker and bring to pressure.

Paleo Pressure Cooker Breakfast Custard Cups
(Servings: 4)

INGREDIENTS:

4 cold large eggs
2 cups coconut milk
1/4 cup sugar
2 tsp. vanilla extract
1/8 tsp. salt
¼ tsp. grated nutmeg

INSTRUCTIONS:

•Pour 2 cups of water into the pressure cooker.
•Whisk the eggs along with the coconut milk, vanilla, sugar and salt in a bowl.
•Distribute the mixture among four 1-cup ramekins that are heat safe.
•Sprinkle the nutmeg on top and cover with a foil.
•Place in a steamer basket and place in the pressure cooker.
•Cover the pressure cooker and set to high heat.
•Bring to 15PSI pressure and then reduce the heat.
•Cook for 5 minutes and then release the pressure using the quick release method.
•Open the lid, and place the ramekins on a wire rack to cool.
•Remove the foil, chill and then serve.

Paleo Pressure Cooker Breakfast Sausage & Potato Hash
(Servings: 4-6)

INGREDIENTS:

1 tbsp. olive oil
½ lb. sweet Italian sausage meat
1 large yellow onion, chopped
1 ½ lbs. medium sweet potatoes, peeled, quartered & thinly sliced
2 tbsp. Worcestershire sauce
½ tsp. ground black pepper
¼ tsp. salt
1 (14-oz.) can diced tomatoes with chiles
¼ cup chicken broth
Fried eggs

INSTRUCTIONS:

•Heat oil in the pressure cooker over medium flame.
•Crumble in the sausage and cook, frequently stirring till browned and then transfer to a bowl.
•Sauté the onions until browned and then stir in the potatoes, pepper, salt, Worcestershire sauce and the sausages.
•Add the tomatoes along with the juice and add the broth.
•Cover the pressure cooker and set to high heat.
•Bring to 15PSI pressure and then reduce the heat.
•Cook for 10 minutes and then release the pressure using the quick release method.
•Open the lid, and place over medium flame and bring to full simmer.
•Cook for 5 minutes until the liquid boils and the bottom of the hash browns.
•If desired place a fried egg over each serving.

Paleo Pressure Cooker Breakfast Corned Beef Hash
(Servings: 4-6)

INGREDIENTS:

3 tbsp. almond butter
1 medium yellow onion, chopped
1 lb. cooked corned beef, diced
2 tsp. minced garlic
1 lb. sweet potatoes, diced
1 small red bell pepper, stemmed, cored and diced
½ tsp. dried thyme
½ tsp. celery seeds
¼ tsp. cayenne
½ cup chicken broth

INSTRUCTIONS:

•Melt the almond butter in the pressure cooker over medium flame.
•Sauté the onions until soft and then stir in the corned beef and the garlic.
•Heat for 2 minutes and then mix in the potatoes, thyme, bell pepper, cayenne, celery seeds and pour in the broth.
•Cover the pressure cooker and set to high heat.
•Bring to 15PSI pressure and then reduce the heat.
•Cook for 10 minutes and then release the pressure using the quick release method.
•Open the lid, and place over medium flame and press the mixture with the back of a wooden spoon without mashing the potatoes.
•Cook for 5 minutes until the mixture dries and begins to brown.

Paleo Pressure Cooker Breakfast Hash with Turkey Sausage & Cranberries
(Servings: 4-6)

INGREDIENTS:

2 tbsp. almond butter
¾ lb. bulk Italian turkey sausage
½ red onion, chopped
½ cup dried cranberries
¼ cup shelled green pumpkin seeds
½ tsp. ground cumin

½ tsp. mild paprika
½ tsp. dried sage
½ tsp. salt
2 medium sweet potatoes, peeled, halved lengthwise and cut widthwise
½ cup chicken broth

INSTRUCTIONS:

•Melt the almond butter in the pressure cooker over medium flame.
•Crumble in the sausage and cook along with the onions until browned, stirring often.
•Mix in the pumpkin seeds, cranberries, cumin, sage, salt, paprika and cayenne and stir cook until it releases an aroma.
•Add and stir fry the potatoes for a minute and pour in the chicken broth.
•Cover the pressure cooker and set to high heat.
•Bring to 15PSI pressure and then reduce the heat.
•Cook for 5 minutes and then release the pressure using the quick release method.
•Open the lid, and place over medium flame.
•Cook for 4 minutes until the mixture dries and begins to brown.

Paleo Pressure Cooker Breakfast Cinnamon Honey Applesauce Spread
(Servings: 6-8)

INGREDIENTS:

¾ cup unsweetened apple juice
3 lbs. medium tart baking apples, cored, peeled and chopped
1/3 cup honey
1 tbsp. fresh lemon juice
½ tsp. ground cinnamon
½ tsp. salt

INSTRUCTIONS:

•Combine all the ingredients in a pressure cooker.
•Cover the pressure cooker and set to high heat.
•Bring to 15PSI pressure and then reduce the heat.
•Cook for 4 minutes and then reduce the pressure naturally.

•Open the lid, and using an immersion blender puree the mixture into a thick sauce.
•Serve spread on toasted Paleo slice bread.

Paleo Pressure Cooker Breakfast Cherry & Apricot Compote
(Servings: 6-8)

INGREDIENTS:

¾ lb. dried apricots, halved
1 lb. fresh sweet cherries, pitted
½ cup sugar
2 tbsp. fresh lemon juice
1 (4-inch) cinnamon stick
¼ tsp. vanilla extract
¼ tsp. salt
1¼ cup water

INSTRUCTIONS:

•Combine all the ingredients in a pressure cooker and stir mix.
•Cover the pressure cooker and set to high heat.
•Bring to 15PSI pressure and then reduce the heat.
•Cook for 8 minutes and then reduce the pressure naturally.
•Open the lid, and discard the cinnamon stick.
•Cool for 15 minutes.

Paleo Pressure Cooker Breakfast Tomato Chutney Tortillas
INGREDIENTS:

4 lbs. ripe tomatoes, pureed
1 (1 inch) piece fresh ginger root, pureed with the tomatoes
Cloves of garlic
½ cup honey
1 cup red wine vinegar
2 onions, cubed
¼ cup golden raisins
¾ tsp. ground cinnamon
½ tsp. ground coriander
¼ tsp. ground cloves
¼ tsp. ground nutmeg
¼ tsp. ground ginger
1 tsp. chili powder
1 pinch paprika
1 tbsp. curry paste
Paleo-friendly tortillas

INSTRUCTIONS:

•Combine all the ingredients in a pressure cooker and stir mix.
•Cover the pressure cooker and for 10 minutes cook at low pressure.
•Reduce the pressure naturally.
•Open the lid, and chill in the refrigerator.
•Place a portion of the chutney at the center of the tortillas and roll it up.

Paleo Pressure Cooker Breakfast Stewed Fruits
(Servings: 6)

INGREDIENTS:

1 cup red wine
1 cup water
½ cup sugar
1 cinnamon stick
2 lemon slices
1 lb. mixed dried fruits

INSTRUCTIONS:

•Combine the wine, water, sugar, lemon slices and cinnamon stick in the pressure cooker and bring to boil, cooking until the sugar dissolves.

- Add the fruits and cover the pressure cooker.
- Bring to 15 PSI pressure on high heat and then reduce the heat once the pressure is reached.
- Cook for 4 minutes.
- Reduce the pressure naturally.
- Open the lid, and transfer to serving bowls.

Paleo Pressure Cooker Breakfast Chops

INGREDIENTS:

35 oz. Mutton chops
17 oz. Potatoes, (Boiled and Mashed)
2 Eggs , beaten
3 Green chilies, finely chopped
2 tbsp. Fresh Coriander Leaves, finely chopped
1/2 cup Grated Paleo Cheddar cheese
Flax meal as required
Oil for frying
1 tbsp. Chicken stock cube, crushed
1 tbsp. Red chili powder
1/2 tsp. Chaat Masala
1 tbsp. Ginger garlic paste
½ tbsp. Coarsely crushed Black pepper
Salt to taste
Olive oil

INSTRUCTIONS:

- Marinate the mutton chops with the red chili powder, salt, ginger garlic paste and pepper for an hour.
- Place the marinated chops in the pressure cooker and cook until tender with half cup water.
- Release the pressure quickly and cook on medium flame uncovered until the liquid dries up..
- Add the cheese, coriander leaves, green chillies, chaat masala, chicken stock cube, salt and pepper to the potatoes and combine well.
- Cover the chops with the mashed potatoes, leaving only the bone uncovered.
- Dip the coated chops in egg and then in the flax meal.
- Shallow fry in heated olive oil, until golden brown.

Paleo Pressure Cooker Mixed Berry Jam

INGREDIENTS:

16 oz. cranberries, washed
16 oz. strawberries, hulled and chopped
8 oz. blueberries, washed
4 oz. dried black raisins
Zest of 1 lemon
45 oz. white sugar
¼ cup water
A pinch of salt

INSTRUCTIONS:

•Place the strawberries, cranberries, raisins, blueberries and lemon zest in a pressure cooker.
•Mix in the sugar and leave for an hour.
•Add the salt and the water and place the cooker on medium flame and bring to boil, stirring often.
•Close the pressure cooker and bring to pressure.
•Once the pressure is reached, reduce the heat and cook for 10 minutes.
•Remove the cooker from the flame and release the pressure naturally.
•Uncover the lid and place on medium flame and bring to boil.
•Boil for 3 minutes, stirring often until it gels and then remove from the flame.
•Skim off the foam, cool and transfer into jars.
•Refrigerate.

Paleo Pressure Cooker Ginger & Rhubarb Breakfast Compote
INGREDIENTS:

½ cup water
1 lb. rhubarb, chopped into 2 inch pieces
½ pint strawberries
¼ cup crystalline ginger, chopped
Honey, to taste

INSTRUCTIONS:

•Pour water into a pressure cooker and bring to boil.
•Add the rhubarb, strawberries and ginger and cover the cooker.
•Bring to high pressure and then turn off the heat.
•Leave to release the pressure naturally.
•Uncover the pressure cooker and stir in some honey to taste.
•Chill.

Paleo Pressure Cooker Apple Breakfast Compote
INGREDIENTS:

1 lb. apples, cut into quarters around the core
½ cup water
1 cup mixed dried cherries and peaches
1 cinnamon stick

INSTRUCTIONS:

•Pour water into a pressure cooker along with the apples, cinnamon stick and dried cherries and peaches.
•Bring to simmer.
•Cover the pressure cooker and bring to pressure.
•Cook for a minute and then turn off the heat.
•Leave to release the pressure naturally.
•Discard the cinnamon stick and chill.

Paleo Pressure Cooker Spiced Fresh Fruit Compote

INGREDIENTS:

1 cup water
1/3 cup orange juice
1/3 cup sugar
1/4 cup dried cherries
Juice and zest of 1 lemon
4 whole allspice berries
4 whole cloves
5 cups mixed fruit, cut in bite-sized pieces
Fresh mint sprigs for garnish

INSTRUCTIONS:

•Place all the ingredients in a pressure cooker except the mint and fresh fruit.
•Cover the pressure cooker and bring to pressure over high heat.
•Cook for a minute and then turn off the heat.
•Release the pressure using the quick release method.
•Add the fresh fruit when the syrup is hot.
•Chill for an hour.

Paleo Chicken Pressure Cooker Recipes

Paleo Pressure Cooker Chicken & Mushroom Soup

INGREDIENTS:

1 whole chicken
Enough water to cover the chicken
1 onion, quartered
2 carrots, trimmed and broken into chunks
2 stalks of celery, broken into chunks
1 lb. crimini mushrooms
1 can organic, peeled tomatoes, cut into large chunks
24-48 white or red pearl onions, peeled
Salt and pepper to taste
Coconut Oil

INSTRUCTIONS:

•Add all the ingredients except the mushrooms to the pressure cooker and cook on high till the pressure cooker hisses loudly.
•Reduce the flame and cook for an hour.
•Sauté the mushrooms in a pan with some coconut oil and place aside.
•Remove the pressure cooker from the heat and allow cold water to flow over it to de-pressurize it.
•Strain the chicken and the vegetables and place the broth in a pot. Discard the veggies.
•Separate the chicken from the bones and add to the broth, discarding the bones.
•Add the mushrooms to the broth as well and reheat the soup.
•Season with salt and pepper.

Paleo Pressure Cooker Barbeque Chicken
(Servings: 4)

INGREDIENTS:

3 chicken breast halves
1 tsp. nutmeg
1 tsp. cinnamon
1/2 tsp. ginger
2 tsp. salt
1/8 tsp. freshly ground pepper
1 ½ cup beer
½ cup water
2 tsp. chicken bouillon
Barbecue sauce of choice

INSTRUCTIONS:

•Combine the cinnamon, nutmeg, ginger, pepper and salt in a bowl and rub it over the chicken pieces.
•Mix the water, beer and chicken bouillon in another bowl and transfer it into the pressure cooker.
•Add the chicken pieces and cover.
•Cook for 20 minutes at 15 PSI.
•Using the natural release technique, release the pressure.
•Remove the chicken and place on the grill cooking for 10 minutes.
•Brush the chicken with the barbeque sauce.
•Grill for another 5 minutes.

Paleo Pressure Cooker Gingery Chicken
(Servings: 4)

INGREDIENTS:

1 chicken cut into pieces
1 large onion - finely diced
1 good piece of fresh ginger - finely grated
¼ cup dry sherry
¼ cup coconut aminos
¼ cup water
Salt and pepper to taste

INSTRUCTIONS:

•Heat some oil in an open pressure cooker and then add the chicken pieces and brown them.
•Add the onion and ginger and mix well.
•Pour in the water, sherry and coconut aminos.
•Close the pressure cooker and heat on high until full pressure is reached.
•Reduce the flame and cook at 10 PSI for 8 minutes.
•Season with salt and pepper.

Paleo Pressure Cooker Cacciatore Chicken
(Servings: 4)

INGREDIENTS:

3 tsp. olive oil
3 shallots, chopped
1 green bell pepper, seeded and coarsely chopped
10oz mushrooms, sliced
3 garlic cloves, chopped
5-6 skinless chicken breasts, halved
2 cups crushed tomatoes
6 tsp. tomato paste
6oz pitted black olives
½ cup dry white wine
Salt and ground black pepper, to taste

INSTRUCTIONS:

•Sauté the onions and bell pepper in olive oil in a pressure cooker for 2 minutes.
•Pour in the dry wine and bring to boil until it is reduced to half.
•Add the garlic and mushrooms and sauté for 3 minutes.
•Place the chicken on top and add the crushed tomatoes over it.
•Layer the tomato paste on top. Do not stir.
•Close the pressure cooker and heat on high until full pressure is reached.
•Reduce the flame and cook for 10 minutes until the chicken is tender.
•Remove from the flame and leave until the pressure releases naturally.
•Open the lid and stir in the olives.
•Season with pepper and salt.

Paleo Pressure Cooker Garlic & Rosemary Chicken
INGREDIENTS:

3 lbs. chicken skinned and cut into pieces
2 tbsp. coconut oil
Salt and pepper to taste
1 tsp. rosemary
4 cloves garlic, peeled and sliced
1/2 cup white cooking wine
1/2 cup chicken broth
1/2 cup water
1/4 cup chopped parsley
1/2 lemon, thinly sliced for garnish

INSTRUCTIONS:

•Heat the coconut oil in the pressure cooker and brown the pieces of chicken.
•Season the chicken with rosemary, salt and pepper.
•Add the garlic.
•Mix all the remaining ingredients in a bowl except the lemon slices and pour over the chicken.
•Close the pressure cooker and place the pressure regulator on the pipe.
•With the pressure regulator rocking gradually, cook for 8 minutes.
•Remove from the flame and allow cold water to flow over the pressure cooker to cool it down.
•If desired thicken the gravy and garnish with lemon.

Paleo Pressure Cooker Chicken Breasts
INGREDIENTS:

3 chicken breasts, cut in half
2 tbsp. coconut oil
Salt and pepper
Paprika
1 tbsp. minced onion
1 carrot
1 1/2 cup strained tomatoes
1 cup water
4 1/2 oz. can button mushrooms, drained

INSTRUCTIONS:

•Heat the coconut oil in the pressure cooker and brown the pieces of chicken.
•Add the onion, carrot, tomatoes, paprika, salt, pepper and water.
•Close the pressure cooker and place the pressure regulator on the pipe.
•With the pressure regulator rocking gradually, cook for 8 minutes.
•Remove from the flame and let the pressure drop naturally.
•Add the mushrooms and place the pressure cooker on the flame.
•Cook for a couple of minutes uncovered and then remove.

Paleo Pressure Cooker Chicken Chasseur
INGREDIENTS:

3 lbs. chicken places
1 lb. tomatoes, chopped
2 tbsp. almond butter
2/3 cup chicken stock
2 tbsp. olive oil
1/2 cup dry white wine
2 small onions, chopped
1 tbsp. tarragon, chopped
1 clove garlic, minced
1 tbsp. parsley, chopped
1/4 lb. fresh mushrooms, sliced
2 tbsp. coconut flour
1/2 cup coconut cream

INSTRUCTIONS:

• Heat the olive oil and almond butter in the pressure cooker and brown the chicken pieces in it.
• Remove the chicken and place aside.
• Add the onions and garlic and sauté until golden brown.
• Add in the mushrooms and cook for a minute.
• Add the chicken back in along with tomatoes, tarragon, wine, parsley and stock.
• Close the pressure cooker and cook for 15 minutes.
• Leave the cooker to de-pressurize naturally and then open.
• Remove the chicken and place on the serving dish.
• Mix the coconut cream and the coconut flour and add it to the gravy in the pressure cooker and mix.
• Cook over medium flame uncovered until thickened, stirring continuously.
• Pour the gravy over the chicken.

Paleo Pressure Cooker Chicken Stock
(Servings: 8)

INGREDIENTS:

1 chicken carcass
1 large carrot
1 large onion
10 cloves garlic
1 stalk celery
15 whole black peppercorns
3 - 4 liters cold water

INSTRUCTIONS:

• Add all the ingredients to the pressure cooker, pouring the water until it reaches the two-thirds mark.
• Cover the pressure cooker and over high flame bring to full pressure.
• Reduce the flame and cook for 30 minutes.
• Remove from the flame and use the natural release method for releasing the pressure.
• Remove the lid and strain the stock.
• Discard the veggies and bones.
• Refrigerate the stock for later use.

Paleo Pressure Cooker Chicken & Dumpling Casserole
(Servings: 4)

INGREDIENTS:

8 chicken thighs, boneless and skinless
2 cups chicken broth
1 cup dry wine
2 tsp. minced garlic (about 4 cloves)
2 cups Paleo friendly biscuit mix
2/3 cup skim milk
1 tbsp. dried dill

INSTRUCTIONS:

•Place the chicken thighs, wine, broth and garlic in the cooker and cook covered on high pressure for 6 minutes.
•Reduce the pressure by placing the cooker under flowing cold water.
•Combine the milk, biscuit mix and dill in a bowl and transfer in spoonfuls in the hot broth.
•Cook for another 6 minutes uncovered.

Paleo Pressure Cooker Herbed Lemon Chicken
(Servings: 4-6)

INGREDIENTS:

1 (3-lb.) chicken, cut up
Salt and pepper
2 - 4 tbsp. olive oil
1 onion, chopped
1 tbsp. chopped garlic
1 cup chicken broth
1/4 cup lemon juice
1 cup chopped parsley
1/2 cup chopped celery leaves
2 tsp. chopped fresh oregano
1 tsp. chopped fresh basil
1 cup pitted black olives
2 tbsp. coconut flour
2 tbsp. cold water

INSTRUCTIONS:

- Season the chicken with salt and pepper.
- Heat oil in a pressure cooker and sauté the onion and garlic and place aside.
- Brown the chicken pieces in batches and place aside.
- Add all the chicken back to the pressure cooker along with the onion and garlic.
- Add the rest of the ingredients other than the water, flour and olives.
- Close the pressure cooker and place the pressure regulator on the vent pipe.
- Cook at 15 lbs. pressure for 8 minutes, with the regulator rocking slowly.
- Cool the pressure cooker by placing under cold water.
- Place the chicken in the serving dish and add the olives to the gravy in the pressure cooker and heat uncovered.
- Mix the cold water and the flour together and pour in into the hot broth.
- Stir cook until thickened and pour the gravy over the chicken.

Paleo Pressure Cooker Tandoori Chicken
INGREDIENTS:

1 medium white onion
1 medium chicken, chopped into pieces with skin removed
6 cloves garlic
1 tsp. ground cloves
1 1/2 tsp. turmeric
1 tsp. coriander
2 tsp. garam masala
1 tsp. salt
Pinch of freshly ground pepper
1 tbsp. honey
1 pint non fat coconut milk yogurt
1 tsp. orange food coloring

INSTRUCTIONS:

- Cut the garlic and onion and blend it in a blender.
- Add the honey with the dry ingredients to the blender and blend.
- Pour the blended mixture in a bowl and blend in the yoghurt and food coloring.
- Add the chicken to the bowl and completely cover with the marinade.
- Marinate the chicken for 2 days.

•Add the chicken to the pressure cooker and cook for 10 minutes on high until ready.

Paleo Pressure Cooker Garlic Vinegar Chicken
(Servings: 4)

INGREDIENTS:

1-1 1/2 lbs. boneless skinless chicken breasts , chopped into chunks
1 large onion, diced
4 cloves garlic, diced
3-4 tbsp. olive oil
1/2 cup water
1/4 cup red wine vinegar
1/2 tsp. basil
2 tbsp. sun-dried tomatoes, chopped
1 tbsp. coconut flour
4 tbsp. cold water
Salt and pepper to taste

INSTRUCTIONS:

•Heat oil in the pressure cooker and brown the chicken.
•Remove the chicken and place aside.
•Heat more oil and sauté the onion and garlic in it.
•Add the chicken and the rest of the ingredients except the cold water and coconut flour.
•Close the pressure cooker and bring to pressure.
•Cook for 8 minutes.
•Mix the flour into the cold water until blended well and then stir into the cooker.

Paleo Pressure Cooker Cracked Pepper Chicken
(Servings: 4)

INGREDIENTS:

  2 chicken breasts, boned, skinned, and cut in half
  2 tsp. cracked mixed peppercorns
  2 tbsp. olive oil
  1/4 cup chopped chives
  1 small garlic clove, minced
  2 tbsp. brandy, optional
  1 cup chicken broth
  1/4 cup flax meal
  1 tbsp. lemon juice
  1 tsp. Worcestershire sauce
  1 tbsp. chopped parsley

INSTRUCTIONS:

•Rub the pepper over the chicken, pressing it into the flesh.
•Heat oil in a pressure cooker and brown the chicken in it.
•Remove the chicken and add the chives, brandy, garlic and broth to the cooker, stirring well.
•Place the steamer basket in the pressure cooker and place the chicken in the steamer basket.
•Close the pressure cooker and place the regulator on the vent pipe.
•Cook for 3-4 minutes with the pressure regulator rocking slowly.
•Cool the cooker and remove the chicken and place in a serving bowl.
•Remove the steamer basket and mix the flax meal, lemon juice, parsley and Worcestershire sauce into the broth.
•Thicken the sauce by heating over the flame and then pour over the chicken.

Paleo Pressure Cooker French Chicken
(Servings: 4-6)

INGREDIENTS:

1 (3-lb.) chicken, cut up
1 onion, sliced
1 carrot, sliced
3 tbsp. coconut flour
1/2 tsp. salt
1/4 tsp. pepper
4 slices bacon
1/2 lb. mushrooms, sliced
1 cup red wine
1 clove garlic, minced
2 tsp. minced parsley
1 tsp. chopped fresh basil
1 small bay leaf
1 (1-lb.) can white onions, drained
1/4 cup brandy

INSTRUCTIONS:

•Mix the coconut flour, salt and pepper in a bowl and coat the onion, carrot and chicken with it.
•Fry the bacon in a pressure cooker until crispy and then crumble and place aside in a bowl.
•Sauté the mushrooms in the bacon drippings left in the pressure cooker and place aside in a bowl.
•Brown the chicken in batches and set aside.
•Brown the onions and carrots and then return the chicken back to the pressure cooker.
•Mix the wine, parsley, basil, garlic and bay leaf in a bowl and pour it over the chicken.
•Close the pressure cooker and place the regulator on the vent pipe.
•Cook at 15 lbs. pressure for 8 minutes with the pressure regulator rocking slowly.
•Cool the pressure cooker immediately and transfer the chicken and veggies into a warm bowl.
•Add the canned onions and mushrooms to the broth and simmer until heated uncovered.
•Add in the bacon and brandy and heat.
•Pour the sauce over the chicken and veggies.

Paleo Pressure Cooker Italian Chicken
(Servings: 2)

INGREDIENTS:

2 chicken breasts, cubed
1 tsp. olive oil
4 cloves of garlic, coarse chopped
1 tsp. salt
1/2 jar any Italian sauce
1 cup water

INSTRUCTIONS:

•Heat oil in a pressure cooker and brown the chicken in it.
•Add the rest of the ingredients and close the pressure cooker.
•Increase the pressure and leave to cook for 30 minutes.
•Allow natural release of pressure and then open the pressure cooker and mix the ingredients well.

Paleo Pressure Cooker Apricot Chicken Casserole
(Servings: 6)

INGREDIENTS:

6 chicken breasts halves
1 1/2 cup water, well seasoned with
Salt to taste
Freshly ground pepper
29 oz. can apricot halves
1 cup apricot nectar
5 tbsp. brandy

INSTRUCTIONS:

•Cook the chicken in a pressure cooker with the water for 8 minutes after the pressure is reached.
•Release the pressure and then place the chicken in a single layer in a casserole dish and place the apricot halves in a layer on top.
•Mix the apricot nectar and the chicken broth present in the pressure cooker.
•Pour the liquid over the chicken and bake covered for 15-20 minutes in an oven pre- heated to 350 degrees Fahrenheit.
•Stir in the brandy just prior to serving.

Paleo Pressure Cooker Herb Roast Chicken

INGREDIENTS:

   3 lbs. Chicken, cut into serving pieces
   3 medium tomatoes, sliced
   1/4 cup parsley, chopped
   1 1/4 cup chicken broth
   1 tbsp. fresh rosemary
   1 tbsp. fresh sage, chopped
   Parsley, chopped
   Salt and pepper to taste
   3-4 tbsp. Olive oil

INSTRUCTIONS:

•Heat oil in a pressure cooker and brown the chicken in it and place aside.
•Add the onions and sauté till golden brown.
•Add the chicken back along with the rest of the ingredients and close the pressure cooker.
•Bring to high pressure.
•Reduce the flame and cook for 15 minutes.
•Release the pressure, uncover and transfer to a serving bowl.

Paleo Pressure Cooker Pineapple Chicken
(Servings: 6)

INGREDIENTS:

   3 lbs. chicken, cut into serving pieces and skinned
   1 tbsp. coconut oil
   20-oz can pineapple chunks, drained and juice reserved
   1 cup reserved juice
   1/2 cup sliced celery
   1 red pepper, cut into chunks
   1/4 cup honey
   1/2 cup vinegar
   2 tbsp. coconut aminos
   1 tbsp. catsup
   1/2 tsp. Worcestershire sauce
   1/4 tsp. ground ginger
   2 tbsp. tapioca starch
   2 tbsp. cold water

INSTRUCTIONS:

•Heat oil in a pressure cooker and brown the chicken in it.
•Mix the pineapple juice with the rest of the ingredients except the pineapple chunks, water and tapioca starch and pour over the chicken.
•Close the pressure cooker and place the regulator on the vent pipe.
•Cook for 8 minutes, with the regulator rocking slightly.
•Release the pressure and transfer the chicken and veggies in a warm dish.
•Mix the tapioca starch in the water and then stir mix it with the liquid in the pressure cooker.
•Cook, stirring constantly, until it thickens.
•Throw in the pineapple chunks and lightly heat.
•Pour the pineapple sauce over the chicken.

Paleo Pressure Cooker Curried Chicken
(Servings: 4-6)

INGREDIENTS:

3 lbs. chicken pieces
2 tbsp. oil
2 tsp. curry powder
Salt to taste
2 onions, chopped
1 tsp. vinegar
1¼ cup water
2 tbsp. coconut flour

INSTRUCTIONS:

•Heat oil in a pressure cooker and brown the chicken in it.
•Season the chicken with the curry powder combined with salt.
•Add the vinegar, 1 cup water and onions.
•Close the pressure cooker and place the regulator on the vent pipe.
•Cook for 10 minutes, with the regulator rocking slightly.
•Release the pressure and transfer the chicken in a warm dish.
•Mix the coconut flour in a ¼ cup of water and then stir mix it with the liquid in the pressure cooker.
•Cook, stirring constantly, until it thickens.
•Pour the sauce over the chicken.

Paleo Pressure Cooker Moroccan Chicken
(Servings: 6)

INGREDIENTS:

1 (2 lb.)butternut squash, peeled and chopped into chunks
3 carrots, cut into ½ inch pieces
1 tbsp. olive oil
3-4 lb. chicken, cut up
3 onions, 3/4 sliced
3 cloves garlic, minced
1 tbsp. grated ginger
2 tsp. ground cumin
2 tsp. ground coriander
Salt & cayenne pepper
1/2 cup raisins
¼ cup water

INSTRUCTIONS:

•Heat oil in a pressure cooker and brown the chicken in it and place aside.
•Add the onions and sauté until golden brown.
•Add the ginger, garlic, salt, pepper and spices and cook for a minute, stirring constantly.
•Add the water, squash and chicken.
•Close the pressure cooker, bring the pressure up.
•Reduce the flame and cook for 15 minutes.
•Release the pressure and then open the lid.
•Mix in the carrots and raisins, close the lid and bring to pressure.
•Reduce the flame and cook for 5 minutes.

Paleo Pressure Cooker Fried Chicken

INGREDIENTS:

1 cup coconut flour
1/2 tsp. pepper
1/2 tsp. flavored pepper
1/2 tsp. poultry seasoning
1/2 tsp. flavored tenderizer
1/2 tsp. onion powder
1/4 tsp. garlic powder
3 eggs
1/2 cup coconut milk
1 tbsp. honey
1 medium chicken, chopped into pieces

INSTRUCTIONS:

•Combine all the dry ingredients in a bowl.
•Cover the chicken pieces with the dry ingredient mix.
•Mix the coconut milk, eggs and honey.
•Sip the chicken in the egg mixture and then coat the chicken pieces again in the dry mix.
•Heat oil in a pressure cooker and brown the chicken.
•Close the pressure cooker and then cook for 15 minutes over medium flame after the pressure is up.

Paleo Pressure Cooker Jardinière Chicken

INGREDIENTS:

6 oz. boneless, skinless chicken breasts, cut into 1 inch cubes
2 medium sweet potatoes, quartered
2 carrots, cut in chunks
2 turnips, quartered
2 stalks celery, cut in chunks
1 medium onion, quartered
1/2 tsp. chicken broth granules
1/2 cup water

INSTRUCTIONS:

•Spray the pressure cooker with a cooking spray.
•Brown the chicken and place aside.
•Place the rack inside the pressure cooker and place all the ingredients including the chicken on top of the rack.
•Close the pressure cooker and bring up the pressure.
•Cook for 4-5 minutes and then cool the pressure immediately by running under cold water.

Paleo Pressure Cooker Tahiti Chicken
(Servings: 4)

INGREDIENTS:

4 chicken breasts
Paprika
4 tbsp. cooking oil
2 (6 oz.) cans frozen pineapple-orange juice concentrate
1/2 cup almond butter
2 tsp. ginger
2 tsp. coconut aminos

INSTRUCTIONS:

•Season the chicken breasts with paprika.
•Heat oil in a pressure cooker and add the chicken.
•Mix the juice, almond butter, ginger and coconut aminos and heat it in a saucepan until well blended.
•Pour the sauce over the chicken and close the pressure cooker.
•Place the regulator on the vent pipe and cook for 10 minutes.

Paleo Pressure Cooker Oriental Chicken
INGREDIENTS:

4 chicken thighs, skin & fat removed
2 tbsp. coconut aminos
1 tsp. honey
1/2 cup celery, sliced
1/4 cup onion, chopped
4 oz. water chestnuts, drained & rinsed
1 (8 oz.) pkg. fresh mushrooms, washed & sliced
3/4 cup water
1/4 tsp. garlic powder
1/4 tsp. dried red pepper flakes
1 tsp. tapioca starch, mixed with 2 tbsp. cold water

INSTRUCTIONS:

•Combine all the ingredients in the pressure cooker except the tapioca starch.
•Close the pressure cooker and place the pressure gauge.
•Bring the cooker up to pressure and then cook for 6 minutes.
•Release the pressure naturally.
•Remove the lid and mix in the tapioca starch mixture and simmer until it thickens

Paleo Pressure Cooker Viennese Chicken
INGREDIENTS:

1 chicken, cut into serving pieces
1 - 2 tbsp. coconut oil
1 onion, chopped
1 bell pepper, chopped
2 - 3 carrots
1 - 2 tomatoes, chopped
4 oz. can mushrooms, drained
1/2 cup chicken bouillon
Salt and pepper to taste
3/4 cup coconut cream
1 tbsp. coconut flour

INSTRUCTIONS:

•Heat the oil in the pressure cooker and brown the chicken pieces.
•Add all the ingredients to the pressure cooker except the cream and the flour.

•Close the pressure cooker and cook for 10 minutes at 15 lbs. of pressure.
•Release the pressure naturally.
•Place the chicken and veggies in a serving dish.
•Blend the cream and flour into the liquid in the pressure cooker and stir cook until it thickens.
•Pour the sauce over the chicken and serve.

Paleo Pressure Cooker Asian Chicken
(Servings: 4)

INGREDIENTS:

1/2 cup slivered almonds
1 tbsp. olive oil
1 tbsp. toasted sesame oil
4 cloves garlic minced
1 tbsp. minced fresh ginger
1 lb. boneless skinless chicken breasts
1/2 medium onion
2 large carrots, diced
2 celery ribs, diced
1/4 cup hoisin sauce blended with 2 tbsp. water
1 tbsp. coconut aminos

INSTRUCTIONS:

•Toast the almonds.
•Heat oil in a pressure cooker and sauté the ginger and garlic in it.
•Add the chicken and slightly brown it.
•Mix in the rest of the ingredients except the almonds.
•Close the pressure cooker, and bring to pressure.
•Cook for 8 minutes at high pressure.
•Release the pressure naturally.
•Serve garnished with the almonds.

Paleo Beef Pressure Cooker Recipes

Paleo Pressure Cooker Beef Bourguignon
(Servings: 5-6)

INGREDIENTS:

32 oz. round steak, cut into 2-3cm pieces
1 cup dry red wine
1/2 cup beef stock
2 carrots, sliced 1/2 cm thick
3 slices of bacon, sliced into 1 cm pieces
8 oz. fresh mushrooms, quartered
2 tbsp. coconut flour
12 small pearl onions, chopped
1/4 tsp. basil
2 cloves garlic, minced

INSTRUCTIONS:

•Fry the bacon in a pressure cooker.
•Add the onions and sauté for 2 minutes.
•Add in the steak and brown it. It takes around 5 minutes.
•Mix in the coconut flour and blend.
•Pour in the wine, beef stock and add the seasonings.
•Close the pressure cooker and cook for 20 minutes.
•Release the pressure, open and then add the mushrooms and carrots.
•Close the lid and cook for another 5 minutes.

Paleo Pressure Cooker Corned Beef
(Servings: 6)

INGREDIENTS:

70 oz. corned beef brisket, preferably flat-cut
12oz sliced celery
2 small oranges, unpeeled and sliced
2 small onions, sliced thinly
2 garlic cloves, chopped
3 bay leaves, halved
1 tbsp. dill
4 cinnamon sticks, halved
2 cups water

INSTRUCTIONS:

•Soak the corned beef brisket for an hour in water and drain it just prior to cooking.
•Transfer the corned beef brisket to the pressure cooker and add the rest of the ingredients, ensuring that the water covers just the surface of the meat.
•Cover the pressure cooker and place the regulator on the vent pipe.
•Cook the meat for 50 minutes at 15 PSI, with the regulator rocking slowly.
•Release the pressure using the natural release method.
•Place the corned beef on a plate and slice thinly against the grain prior to serving.

Paleo Pressure Cooker Pepper Steak

INGREDIENTS:

2 tbsp. olive oil
1 large onion, sliced
2 cloves garlic, sliced
1 lb. beef round steak, cut into -3 x 1/2
1/2 cup beef broth
1 tbsp. sherry
1 tsp. honey
1/2 tsp. salt
1 tsp. ginger root, grated
1/2 tsp. red pepper flakes
2 tomatoes, cut into eighths
1 green bell pepper, sliced
4 green onions, coarsely chopped
1/4 cup coconut aminos
2 tbsp. water
2 tbsp. tapioca starch

INSTRUCTIONS:

•Heat olive oil in a pressure cooker and sauté garlic and onion in it for 2 minutes.
•Add the beef strips and stir cook on high for a minute.
•Mix in the broth, honey, salt, sugar, pepper flakes and ginger root.
•Close the pressure cooker and raise the pressure on high flame.
•Reduce the flame, maintain the pressure and cook for 10 minutes.
•Release the pressure and uncover.
•Mix in the bell pepper, tomatoes and green onions.
•Close the pressure cooker and raise the pressure on high flame.
•Reduce the flame, maintain the pressure and cook for 2 minutes.
•Release the pressure and uncover.
•Mix the coconut aminos, tapioca starch and water in a bowl, blending until smooth.
•Pour the mixture over the beef and veggies, stirring until creamy and thickened.

Paleo Pressure Cooker Swiss Steak

INGREDIENTS:

2 lbs. beef round steak, 1 inch thick
Olive oil
1 cup water
Salt and pepper
1 onion chopped
1 cup celery, diced
1 green pepper, diced
1 cup tomato juice

INSTRUCTIONS:

•Chop the meat into pieces and season with salt and pepper.
•Heat oil in a cooker and brown the meat.
•Add the rest of the ingredients.
•Close the pressure cooker and cook for 15 minutes, with the pressure regulator rocking.
•Release the pressure and uncover.
•If desired, thicken the sauce.

Paleo Pressure Cooker Beef Tongue

INGREDIENTS:

1 tongue
2 cups water
2 tsp. salt
1 tbsp. chopped parsley
1 bay leaf
1 carrot, sliced
1 onion, sliced

INSTRUCTIONS:

•Place the tongue in the pressure cooker with the rest of the ingredients.
•Close the pressure cooker and cook for 45 minutes after the pressure is up.
•Release the pressure normally.
•Cool the tongue and then peel of the skin.
•Slice and serve.

Paleo Pressure Cooker Beef Spare Ribs with Barbeque Sauce
(Servings: 6)

INGREDIENTS:

3 lbs. spareribs, cut into serving pieces
Salt and pepper
Paprika
1 tbsp. olive oil
1 large onion, sliced
1/4 cup catsup
2 tbsp. vinegar
1 tsp. Worcestershire sauce
1/8 tsp. chili powder
1/4 tsp. celery seed
1 1/2 cup water

INSTRUCTIONS:

•Season ribs with paprika, salt and pepper.
•Heat olive oil in the cooker over medium flame and brown the ribs.
•Throw in the onion.
•Mix the vinegar, catsup, chili powder, Worcestershire sauce, water and celery seed.
•Pour the mixture over the meat.
•Close the pressure cooker and place the pressure regulator on the vent pipe.
•Cook for 15 minutes at 15 lbs. pressure.
•Release the pressure naturally.

Paleo Pressure Cooker Beef Stroganhoff
INGREDIENTS:

2 lbs. beef stew meat, cut into 1" cubes
3 tbsp. olive oil
2 tbsp. coconut flour
1 large onion, chopped
1 tsp. garlic
1 cup beef broth
1/4 lb. fresh mushrooms, sliced
2 tbsp. tomato paste
1 tbsp. Worcestershire sauce
1 cup coconut cream

Salt and pepper to taste

INSTRUCTIONS:

•Heat oil in a cooker and brown the meat.
•Add the coconut flour and mix well.
•Mix in the garlic powder, onions, mushrooms, Worcestershire sauce, salt, pepper and tomato paste.
•Mix well and close the pressure cooker.
•Bring to high pressure and then cook for 20 minutes.
•Release the pressure naturally, open and stir in the cream.

Paleo Pressure Cooker Beefy Tomato Soup
(Servings: 4)

INGREDIENTS:

1 lb. lean beef, sliced
3 cups water
1 large onion, chopped
2 carrot, sliced
1 1/2 cup cabbage, shredded
2 1/4 lbs. tomato, quartered
1 bay leaf
1 clove garlic
1 tsp. lemon juice
1/2 tsp. salt
1/8 tsp. pepper
1 tsp. honey
1 cup coconut cream
2 tbsp. tapioca starch

INSTRUCTIONS:

•Combine all the ingredients in the pressure cooker except the tapioca starch and the cream.
•Close the pressure cooker.
•Bring to high pressure and then cook for 20 minutes.
•Release the pressure naturally, open and remove the bay leaf.
•Combine the cream and tapioca starch with 1 cup of soup and then pour the entire mixture into the rest of the soup in the pressure cooker, stirring continuously.

Paleo Pressure Cooker Chuck Steak with Tomatoes
(Servings: 6-8)

INGREDIENTS:

3 lbs. lean chuck steak, fat trimmed off and chopped into cubes
2 cups canned tomatoes
3 tbsp. olive oil
24 pimiento-stuffed green olives
2 tbsp. garlic, minced
1/2 tsp. dried thyme leaves
2 medium onions, cut into 1-in. cubes
1 bay leaf
1/2 lb. mushrooms, quartered
Pinch of cayenne
1/4 cup coconut flour
1/2 tsp. saffron
1 cup dry red wine
1/4 cup parsley, chopped

INSTRUCTIONS:

•Heat oil in a pressure cooker until smoking and brown the beef cubes over high flame, stirring frequently.
•Add in the onions, garlic and mushrooms.
•Add the coconut flour and mix to coat evenly.
•Add the tomatoes, wine, thyme, olives, cayenne, bay leaf and saffron.
•Bring to boil, stirring constantly.
•Close the pressure cooker and fit the pressure regulator.
•Reduce the flame and cook for 20-25 minutes.
•Release the pressure naturally and open the lid.
•Serve the beef topped with parsley.

Paleo Pressure Cooker Corned Beef with Cabbage
INGREDIENTS:

4 cups water
2 1/2 lbs. corned beef brisket
3 cloves garlic, halved
2 bay leaves
4 carrots cut into 3" pieces
1 head cabbage cut into 6 wedges
6 peeled and quartered sweet potatoes
3 peeled and quartered turnips
Horseradish sauce

INSTRUCTIONS:

•Pour water into a pressure cooker and add the beef brisket to it.
•Bring the water to boil over high flame and skim off the residue from the surface.
•Add in the bay leaves and garlic and close the pressure cooker.
•Bring to high pressure over high flame.
•Reduce the flame to maintain pressure and cook for an hour and 15 minutes.
•Release the pressure naturally and open the lid.
•Add the veggies to the brisket and stir gently.
•Close the pressure cooker and bring to high pressure over high flame.
•Reduce the flame to maintain pressure and cook for 6 minutes.
•Release the pressure naturally and open the lid.
•Serve with horseradish sauce.

Paleo Pressure Cooker Roasted Beef
(Servings: 6)

INGREDIENTS:

2 lbs. lean beef, cubed
1 tsp. olive oil
1 can stewed tomatoes
2 tsp. California chili powder
2 tbsp. tomato paste
1 to 2 cups water
2 tsp. salt
1/2 tsp. oregano

INSTRUCTIONS:

•Heat oil in a pressure cooker and brown the beef.
•Mix in all the rest of the ingredients.
•Close the pressure cooker.
•Bring to high pressure over high flame.
•Reduce the flame to maintain pressure and cook for 45 minutes.
•Release the pressure naturally and open the lid.

Paleo Pressure Cooked Beef Heart
(Servings: 4)

INGREDIENTS:

1 lb. well-trimmed beef heart
1 cabbage leaf
1 onion, sliced in thick rings
1 celery stalk, chopped
1 bay leaf
1 cup water

INSTRUCTIONS:

•Combine all the ingredients in the pressure cooker.
•Close the pressure cooker.
•Bring to high pressure over high flame.
•Reduce the flame to maintain pressure and cook for 45 minutes.
•Release the pressure naturally and open the lid.

Paleo Pressure Cooked Beef & Veggie Soup
(Servings: 6)

INGREDIENTS:

1 lb. lean boneless beef steak, cut into 2 inch cubes with fat trimmed
3 cups beef stock
1/2 cup pared, diced rutabaga
2 carrots, pared in chunks
1 parsnip, pared in chunks
1 lg. rib celery, in 2-inch slices
1 leek, trimmed, cut up
Salt & pepper to taste
2 sweet potatoes, cubed
2 tbsp. parsley, minced

INSTRUCTIONS:

•Combine the water and beef in a pressure cooker and boil.
•Skim off the foam and add all the rest of the ingredients except the parsley and sweet potatoes.
•Close the pressure cooker and bring to high pressure over high flame.
•Reduce the flame to maintain pressure and cook for 40 minutes.
•Release the pressure naturally and open the lid.
•Add the sweet potatoes.
•Close the pressure cooker and bring to high pressure over high flame.
•Reduce the flame to maintain pressure and cook for 5 minutes.
•Release the pressure naturally and open the lid.
•Add the parsley and heat lightly.

Paleo Pressure Cooker Barbeque Beef

INGREDIENTS:

2 lb. cubed beef
1/4 cup water
1 tsp. salt
5 tbsp. honey
2 tbsp. molasses
1/4 cup catsup
1 tsp. mustard
1/2 cup barbecue sauce
1 drop Hickory sauce

INSTRUCTIONS:

•Combine the beef, salt and water in a pressure cooker and cook for 30-35 minutes covered.
•Release the pressure naturally and open the lid.
•Add the rest of the ingredients and leave on flame to thicken slightly.

Paleo Pressure Cooker Beef Cubed Steaks in Gravy

INGREDIENTS:

4 -6 beef cubed steaks
3-4 tbsp. olive oil
Coconut Flour
1 onion, chopped
2 tbsp. catsup
1 beef bouillon cube
Few chopped mushrooms
Seasoned salt
Garlic salt
Salt and pepper
5-6 dashes of Worcestershire sauce
Water
2 dashes coconut aminos

INSTRUCTIONS:

•Coat the steaks with the coconut flour and brown in olive oil in a pressure cooker.
•Sprinkle the seasoned salt, garlic salt, pepper and salt.
•Add the remaining ingredients with sufficient water to cover the steaks.

•Close the pressure cooker and place on high flame until the pressure is up.
•Reduce the flame and cook for 20 minutes
•Cool the pressure cooker under flowing cold water and uncover it.
•Place the steaks on a serving dish.
•Thicken the gravy and pour over the steaks.

Paleo Pressure Cooker Beef Shanks
INGREDIENTS:

3-4 lb. beef shanks
1 pkg. 15 minute marinade
1/3 cup water
1/3 cup sherry
2 tbsp. tomato paste
1/4 tsp. rosemary
1/2 tsp. oregano
6 medium carrots, cut diagonally
12 small onions

INSTRUCTIONS:

•Combine the marinade package with the water, tomato paste, sherry and spices in a bowl.
•Pierce the meat and place in the marinade, turning frequently for a couple of hours.
•Place the meat in the pressure cooker and cook covered for 30-35 minutes at 10 lbs. pressure.
•Release the pressure naturally, open and add the veggies.
•Cook covered for 20-30 minutes at 10 lbs. pressure.
•Release the pressure naturally and open the lid.

Paleo Pressure Cooker Pickled Beef Heart

INGREDIENTS:

1 beef heart
Garlic cloves
Onion, sliced
Whole pickling spice
Cider vinegar
Water

INSTRUCTIONS:

•Rinse the beef heart with cold water and then with a small knife make slits at different points in the beef.
•Fill each slit with a clove of garlic.
•Place the beef in a six-quart pressure cooker and pour the cider vinegar to fill it half.
•Add the sliced onion and a few more garlic cloves.
•Add water to make the cooker three-fourths full and add a handful of pickling spice.
•Cover the pressure cooker and cook on high until the pressure is up.
 •Reduce the flame and cook for 40 minutes.
•Release the pressure naturally and open the lid.
•Remove the beef heart from the pickling liquid, slice and return back to the liquid.
•Store in the refrigerator.

Paleo Pressure Cooker Beef Chili

INGREDIENTS:

2 tbsp. olive oil
2 medium onions chopped
3 cloves garlic minced
1½ lbs. ground beef
2 tsp. ground cumin
2 tbsp. chili powder, or to taste
1½ tsp. oregano
1 bay leaf
2 tsp. celery seed
Salt to taste
1 tbsp. coconut flour
1½ cup crushed tomato
1 cup beef stock

INSTRUCTIONS:

•Heat oil in a pressure cooker and sauté the onions and garlic in it.
•Add the beef and brown it.
•Add in the chili powder, cumin, bay leaf, oregano, celery seeds, flour and salt.
•Mix in the beef stock and crushed tomatoes.
•Cover the pressure cooker and bring to pressure.
 •Cook for 15 minutes at high pressure.
•Release the pressure naturally and open the lid.

Paleo Pressure Cooker Pickled Beef Tongue

INGREDIENTS:

1 beef tongue
Garlic cloves
Onion, sliced
Whole pickling spice
Cider vinegar
Water

INSTRUCTIONS:

•Rinse the beef tongue with cold water and then with a small knife make slits at different points in the beef.
•Fill each slit with a clove of garlic.
•Place the beef in a six-quart pressure cooker and pour the cider vinegar to fill it half.
•Add the sliced onion and a few more garlic cloves.
•Add water to make the cooker three-fourths full and add a handful of pickling spice.
•Cover the pressure cooker and cook on high until the pressure is up.
 •Reduce the flame and cook for 40 minutes.
•Release the pressure naturally and open the lid.
•Remove the beef tongue from the pickling liquid, peel off the skin, slice and return back to the liquid.
•Store in the refrigerator.

Paleo Pressure Cooker Mongolian Beef
(Servings: 6)

INGREDIENTS:

2 lbs. flank steak, cut into 1/4" strips
1 tbsp. olive oil
4 cloves garlic, minced
1/2 cup coconut aminos
1/2 cup water
2/3 cup Muscovado Sugar
1/2 tsp. minced fresh ginger
2 tbsp. tapioca starch
3 tbsp. water
3 green onions, sliced into 1-inch pieces

INSTRUCTIONS:

•Season the meat with salt and pepper.
•Heat oil in a pressure cooker and brown the beef in batches and place aside.
•Sauté the garlic for a minute and then add the coconut aminos, ½ cup water, Muscovado Sugar and ginger, stirring to mix.
•Add the beef back along with the collected juices.
•Select high pressure and set the timer for 12 minutes.
•Once the cooking is complete, turn it off and release the pressure using the quick pressure release.
•Remove the lid.
•Combine the tapioca starch with the 3 tbsp. water and whisk until blended.
•Pour the mixture into the pressure cooker sauce and stir continuously.
•Bring to boil, stirring continuously until the sauce thickens.
•Mix in the green onions.

Paleo Pressure Cooker Asian Boneless Beef Ribs
(Servings: 6)

INGREDIENTS:

1 tbsp. olive oil
4 garlic cloves, minced
1 (2-inch) piece ginger, peeled, sliced into 1/4-inch-thick rounds, and smashed
1/2 cup hoisin sauce
2 tbsp. coconut aminos
2 tbsp. dry sherry
4 scallions, white parts chopped coarse, green parts sliced thin
1/4 tsp. cayenne pepper
6 (8-oz.) boneless beef short ribs, trimmed
2 tbsp. minced fresh cilantro

INSTRUCTIONS:

•Heat oil and cook the ginger and garlic in it until fragrant.
•Add the coconut aminos, hoisin sauce, scallion whites, sherry, cayenne and then the beef.
•Close the pressure cooker, bring to high pressure over high flame.
•Reduce the flame and cook for 35 minutes.
•Release the pressure using the natural release method.
•Place the ribs on a serving dish.
•Strain the sauce in a fat separator, leave for 5 minutes and pour the sauce in a bowl. Mix the scallion greens and cilantro in the sauce.
•Serve the sauce with then ribs.

Paleo Pressure Cooker Beef Curry
(Servings: 4)

INGREDIENTS:

17 ½ oz. diced beef chuck steak
Large glug of olive Oil
2 to 3 large sweet potatoes, diced
2 ½ tbsp. curry powder, mild
1 tbsp. grainy wine mustard
2 large onions, chopped
2 cloves garlic, chopped
1 can of coconut milk
1 jar of tomato sauce

INSTRUCTIONS:

•Heat oil in a pressure cooker and caramelize the onions and garlic in it.
•Add the sweet potatoes and mustard and cook for a minute.
•Add the beef and brown it.
•Mix in the curry powder and stir fry for 2 minutes.
•Pour in the coconut milk and tomato sauce.
•Cover the pressure cooker securely and cook for 10 minutes.

Paleo Pressure Cooker Beef Pot Roast
(Servings: 6-8)

INGREDIENTS:

53 oz. beef chuck roast, excess fat trimmed off
2 cups beef stock
½ cup red wine
½ tsp. salt
½ tsp. black pepper
½ tsp. smoked paprika
½ tsp. chicken salt
1 medium onion, roughly chopped
4 cloves garlic, minced
3 medium carrots, cut into chunks
5 medium sweet potatoes, cut into chunks

INSTRUCTIONS:

•Mix the paprika, chicken salt, salt and pepper in a bowl and rub it over the beef.
•Place the beef in the pressure cooker and add the onion, garlic, red wine and beef stock to it.
•Close the pressure cooker and cook for 45-50 minutes on high.
•Use the quick release method to release the pressure.
•Add the carrots and potatoes, stirring the mixture.
•Close the pressure cooker and return to pressure.
•Cook for an additional 5-10 minutes.
•Use the natural release method to release the pressure.

Paleo Pressure Cooker Thai Curried Beef

INGREDIENTS:

1 jar Thai Red Curry Paste
1 (14 oz.) can of coconut milk
1 tbsp. olive oil
2 medium onions, quartered
1 large red bell pepper, quartered
1 cup water
1 tbsp. honey
1 tbsp. coconut aminos
1 tbsp. fish sauce
3 lbs. beef chuck roast, cut into 1 inch pieces
1 tsp. kosher salt
4 – 6 sweet potatoes
2 tbsp. dried basil

INSTRUCTIONS:

•Heat oil in a pressure cooker and brown the onions and bell pepper in it, until lightly charred. Remove and place aside.
•Add the cream atop the coconut milk can and deglaze the pressure cooker.
•Add the Thai curry paste and mix.
•Cook for 4-6 minutes and then add the rest of the coconut milk and the remaining ingredients along with the browned veggies.
•Close the pressure cooker and bring to pressure on high flame.
•Reduce the flame and cook for 12 minutes.
•Use the natural release method to release the pressure.

Paleo Pressure Cooker Beef Stock

INGREDIENTS:

2 tbsp. tomato paste
3 lbs. meaty beef marrow bones
2 1/2 lbs. (1-inch-thick) beef shanks
2 celery stalks, diagonally cut into 2-inch pieces
1 large carrot, peeled and diagonally cut into 2-inch pieces
1 large onion, peeled and cut into 8 wedges
1 Tbsp. black peppercorns
2 bay leaves
1/2 bunch fresh flat-leaf parsley
8 cups cold water

INSTRUCTIONS:

•Brush the tomato paste over the bones and shanks and place in a roasting pan.
•Add the carrot, celery and onion to the pan and coat lightly with a cooking spray.
•Bake in an oven preheated to 500 degrees Fahrenheit for 30 minutes.
•Transfer the baked mixture into a pressure cooker and throw in the pepper corns, bay leaves and parsley.
•Pour the water in and close the pressure cooker.
•Bring to high pressure over high flame.
•Reduce the flame and cook for 35 minutes.
•Release the pressure through the steam vent and open the lid.
•Allow to stand for 20 minutes and then strain the stock through a sieve lined with cheesecloth into a bowl.
•Press down the solids to remove the excess stock and discard the solids.
•Chill.

Paleo Seafood Pressure Cooker Recipes

Paleo Pressure Cooker Conch Curry

INGREDIENTS:

1 cup conch
2 1/2 cups water
1 tsp. salt
2 cloves garlic
3 stalks scallions
2 tbsp. olive oil
2 tbsp. curry powder
1 tsp. coriander
1 sprig thyme
1 small chayote, chopped into cubes
2 small carrots, chopped into cubes

INSTRUCTIONS:

•Place the water, conch, scallions, garlic and salt in the pressure cooker and cook covered for 25 minutes till the conch is tender.
•Heat the olive oil in a pan and stir in the curry powder for 30 seconds.
•Add in the coriander, thyme and the cooked conch along with the liquid and stir mix.
•Add the carrots and chayote and cook until crispy tender.

Paleo Pressure Cooked Smoked Salmon Zucchini Pasta
(Servings: 6)

INGREDIENTS:

1/4 cup olive oil
2 cups julienned zucchini
4 cups chicken broth
3/4 tsp. salt
1/4 tsp. white pepper
1 tsp. dried thyme
3 tbsp. almond butter, cut into small pieces
1/2 cup coconut cream
1 lb. smoked salmon, separated into bite-size pieces
2 green onions, chopped

INSTRUCTIONS:

•Heat oil in a pressure cooker and add the broth, julienned zucchini, pepper, salt and thyme to it.
•Close the pressure cooker and bring to high pressure.
•Lower the heat and cook for 2 minutes.
•Release the pressure naturally, uncover and drain the zucchini in a colander.
•Place the zucchini in a bowl and toss in the almond butter and coconut cream.
•Add the smoked salmon and green onions and toss together to mix.

Paleo Pressure Cooker Lemongrass & Shrimp Broth
INGREDIENTS:

6 stalks lemongrass, chopped
4 cups loosely packed Chinese celery, chopped
The shells and heads from 4 lbs. of shrimp turned into a shrimp mush
Large handful of fresh cilantro
3 whole scallions, chopped
Root ends from handful leek trimmings

INSTRUCTIONS:

•Chop the lemongrass into 2 inch chunks and bruise it with the back of a heavy knife. Discard the woody brown stems.

•Place the shrimp shells and heads in a blender and cover with a little water and blend into a mush.
•Place all the ingredients in a pressure cooker and fill with water to the maximum fill line.
•Cook covered on high for 15 minutes and then allow the pressure to release naturally.
•Strain the broth into a bowl.

Paleo Pressure Cooked Mustard Halibut Steaks
(Servings: 4)

INGREDIENTS:

4 small halibut steaks, 1-inch thick
4 tbsp. Dijon mustard
4 sprigs fresh thyme
1 tbsp. olive oil
1 onion, chopped
1 garlic clove, minced
1 cup dry white wine
1 bay leaf
2 tbsp. Dijon mustard
1 tbsp. tapioca starch

INSTRUCTIONS:

•Spread mustard on the halibut steaks and press down a sprig of thyme into each steak.
•Heat oil in a pressure cooker and sauté onion and garlic in it.
•Mix in the wine and add the bay leaf.
•Place the steamer basket in the cooker and place the halibut steaks on it.
•Close the pressure cooker and place the pressure regulator on the vent pipe.
•Cook at 15 lbs. pressure for 2 minutes, with the regulator rocking slowly.
•Cool the pressure cooker and remove the salmon steaks and place in a platter.
•Discard the bay leaf and remove the steamer basket.
•Combine the tapioca starch with 2 tbsp. mustard and blend it into the sauce in the cooker.
•Cook until the sauce thickens and then serve with the steaks.

Paleo Pressure Cooker Mediterranean-Style Halibut fish
(Servings: 4)

INGREDIENTS:

4 fillets of halibut fish
17 ½ oz. cherry tomatoes, cut in halves
1 cup Taggiesche olives
1 clove of garlic, pressed
2 tbsp. pickled capers
Olive oil
Thyme
Salt and pepper

INSTRUCTIONS:

•Put the cherry tomatoes at the base of a heatproof bowl and add a bunch of fresh thyme leaves.
•Place the fish fillets on top and then sprinkle the crushed garlic, pickled capers, olives, salt, pepper and olive oil.
•Place the bowl in the pressure cooker and set the cooker to low pressure. Turn the flame to high.
•Reduce the flame and cook for 5 minutes.
•Allow the pressure to release naturally.
•Garnish with cherry tomatoes prior to serving.

Paleo Pressure Cooker Salmon Al Cartoccio
(Servings: 4)

INGREDIENTS:

4 salmon fillets, fresh
3 tomatoes, sliced
1 lemon, sliced
1 white onion, shaved
4 sprigs of parsley
4 sprigs of thyme
Olive oil
Salt and pepper, to taste

INSTRUCTIONS:

•Place all the ingredients on a parchment paper in the order: first a drizzle of oil, a layer of tomatoes, salt, pepper and oil, then 2 fish fillets

followed by salt, pepper, oil, herbs, onion rings, lemon slices and finally with a drizzle of oil and salt.
•Repeat for the remaining 2 fillets.
•Fold the parchment paper and wrap it in a tin foil.
•Put 2 cups of water in a big pressure cooker and keep the steamer basket in place.
•Lay one of the tin foil packets in the basket.
•Place the second layer of steamer basket and put the second tin foil packet in it.
•Close the pressure cooker and turn to high heat until the pressure is reached.
•Turn the heat down and cook for 12-15 minutes.
•Allow the pressure to release naturally.
•Open the lid after 5 minutes.

Paleo Pressure Cooker Coconut Fish Curry
(Servings: 6-8)

INGREDIENTS:

26oz fish fillets, bite-size pieces, rinsed
2 cups unsweetened coconut milk
1 tomato, chopped
2 capsicums, cut into strips
2 onions, cut into strips
2 garlic cloves, squeezed
6 curry leaves
1 tbsp. freshly grated ginger
1 tbsp. ground coriander
1/2 tsp. ground turmeric
2 tsp. ground cumin
1 tsp. hot pepper flakes
1/2 tsp. ground fenugreek
2 tbsp. coconut oil
Salt
Lemon juice

INSTRUCTIONS:

•Heat the pressure cooker and add oil and fry curry leaves in it for a minute.
•Sauté onion, garlic and ginger in the oil and then add turmeric, hot pepper, coriander, cumin, and fenugreek.

•Sauté for 2 minutes and then add coconut milk and deglaze the bottom of the cooker.
•Add the tomatoes, capsicum and fish, coating the fish with the mixture.
•Close the pressure cooker and set a low pressure level and a high heat level.
•Turn the heat down after reaching the pressure and cook for 5 minutes.
•Release the pressure through the valve.
•Season the curry with salt and sprinkle lemon juice on top.

Paleo Pressure Cooker Steamed Haddock Fillets (Servings: 4)

INGREDIENTS:

4 haddock fish fillets
1 cup water
17 oz. cherry tomatoes, sliced
1 cup olives
1 clove of garlic, crushed
A large pinch of fresh thyme
Olive oil
Salt and pepper, to taste

INSTRUCTIONS:

•Heat the pressure cooker and add a cup of water to it.
•Place the fillets in one layer in the steamer basket fitted to the pressure cooker.
•Keep the cherry tomatoes and olives over the fish fillets.
•Sprinkle the garlic, thyme sprigs, olive oil and salt and close the pressure cooker.
•Place on high flame until the pressure is reached and then reduce the heat.
•Cook for 10 minutes at low pressure.
•Release the pressure through the natural release method.
•Season the fillets with pepper and sprinkle some thyme and some oil prior to serving.

Paleo Pressure Cooked Halibut with Ginger & Orange Sauce (Servings: 4)

INGREDIENTS:

4 halibut fish fillets
Juice and zest from 1 orange
Thumb size piece of ginger, chopped
4 spring onions
Olive oil
Salt and pepper
1 cup of white wine

INSTRUCTIONS:

•Dry the fish fillets with a paper towel and rub some olive oil into them.
•Season the fillets with salt and pepper.
•Add the white wine, ginger, orange juice and zest and spring onions to the pressure cooker.
•Put the fish in the steamer basket and close the pressure cooker.
•Heat up to pressure and then cook for 7 minutes.
•After cooking, place the fillets on a serving platter and cover with the sauce

Paleo Pressure Cooked Sweet & Sour Shrimps

INGREDIENTS:

1 lb. small shrimp, peeled
3 tbsp. coconut aminos
2 tbsp. white vinegar
1/2 cup pineapple juice
2 tbsp. sugar
1 cup chicken broth

INSTRUCTIONS:

•Combine all the ingredients in a pressure cooker and cover with the lid.
•Bring to pressure and then lower the heat.
•Cook for 3 minutes.
•Release the pressure naturally.
•If required to thicken the sauce, place on low flame and continuously stir.

Paleo Pressure Cooked Seafood Gumbo
(Servings: 10)

INGREDIENTS:

1/2 tsp. dried thyme
2 tbsp. olive oil
2 onions, coarsely chopped
1 (13 or 14 oz.) can stewed tomatoes, with juice
1 lb. fresh okra, cut into 1/4 inch slices
2 lbs. raw shrimp, shelled and deveined
1/8 tsp. cayenne pepper
4 cups chicken stock
4 cups water
1/4 cup minced fresh parsley
1 bay leaf
3 cloves garlic, minced
1 lb. crab meat
1 lb. chicken breast meat, cubed
1/2 lb. ham, cut into quarter inch cubes

INSTRUCTIONS:

•Heat the oil in a pressure cooker and sauté the onions in it. Remove and drain on paper towels.
•Throw in the chicken cubes and ham and brown it lightly, constantly stirring.
•Transfer the onions back to the cooker and add the water, stock, okra, garlic, thyme, bay leaf, cayenne pepper, parsley and tomatoes along with the liquid.
•Cover the pressure cooker and bring to pressure.
•Lower the heat and cook for 20 minutes.
•Release the pressure naturally.
•Add the crab meat and shrimps and simmer gently uncovered until the shrimps turn pink.

Paleo Pressure Cooked Seafood Bouillabaise

INGREDIENTS:

3 tbsp. olive oil
2 onions, chopped
2 cloves garlic
2 tbsp. parsley, chopped
1 can tomatoes, drained and chopped
1 bay leaf
1 tsp. thyme
1/4 tsp. saffron, crushed
4 cups water
1 lb. hearty fish fillets, cut in chunks
1 lb. lobster tail, cut in chunks
12 oz. scallops
1/4 lb. shrimp, shelled
6 clams in shells
Salt and pepper to taste

INSTRUCTIONS:

•Heat the oil in a pressure cooker and sauté the onions in it.
•Add the tomatoes, parsley, garlic, thyme, saffron, bay leaf, salt, pepper and water.
•Cover the pressure cooker and bring to high pressure.
•Cook for 5 minutes.
•Release the pressure naturally.
•Add the clams, shrimps, scallops fish, lobster tails and stir.
•Cover the pressure cooker and bring to high pressure.
•Cook for 3 minutes.
•Release the pressure naturally, open and serve.

Paleo Pressure Cooked Creole Cod
(Servings: 8)

INGREDIENTS:

1/4 cup olive oil
2 cups chopped onion
1 large green pepper, chopped
1 cup chopped celery
2 cloves garlic, minced
1 (28-oz.) can tomatoes, chopped
1/4 cup white wine
2 (1-lb.) blocks frozen cod fillets
2 bay leaves
1 tbsp. paprika
1/2 tsp. cayenne pepper
1 tsp. salt

INSTRUCTIONS:

•Heat oil in a pressure cooker and sauté the onions, green pepper, garlic and celery in it.
•Remove the veggies and place aside.
•Drain the juice from the tomatoes, around a cup and put the tomato juice and wine in the pressure cooker.
•Place the steamer basket in the pressure cooker and place the two frozen blocks of the fish in a crossed fashion.
•The fish should not go above the two-thirds mark.
•Close the pressure cooker and place the regulator on the vent pipe.
•Cook at 15 lbs. pressure for 5 minutes with the regulator rocking slightly.
•Release the pressure naturally, open and remove the fish.
•Add the sautéed veggies, bay leaves, tomatoes, salt, cayenne pepper and paprika to the juice in the pressure cooker.
•Break the fish into chunks and add it back to the pressure cooker.
•Close the pressure cooker and place the regulator on the vent pipe.
•Cook for 10 minutes at 15 lbs. pressure.
•Cool the cooker and place the fish in a serving dish.
•Discard the bay leaf and pour the sauce over the fish.

Paleo Pressure Cooked Creamy Smoked Trout Zucchini Pasta
(Servings: 6)

INGREDIENTS:

1/4 cup olive oil
2 cups julienned zucchini
4 cups chicken broth
3/4 tsp. salt
1/4 tsp. white pepper
1 tsp. dried thyme
3 tbsp. almond butter, cut into small pieces
1/2 cup coconut cream
1 lb. smoked trout separated into bite-size pieces
2 green onions, chopped

INSTRUCTIONS:

•Heat oil in a pressure cooker and add the broth, julienned zucchini, pepper, salt and thyme to it.
•Close the pressure cooker and bring to high pressure.
•Lower the heat and cook for 2 minutes.
•Release the pressure naturally, uncover and drain the zucchini in a colander.
•Place the zucchini in a bowl and toss in the almond butter and coconut cream.
•Add the smoked trout and green onions and toss together to mix.

Paleo Pressure Cooked Salmon Steaks Moutarde
(Servings: 4)

INGREDIENTS:

4 small salmon steaks, 1-inch thick
4 tbsp. Dijon mustard
4 sprigs fresh thyme
1 tbsp. olive oil
1 onion, chopped
1 garlic clove, minced
1 cup dry white wine
1 bay leaf
2 tbsp. Dijon mustard
1 tbsp. tapioca starch

INSTRUCTIONS:

•Spread mustard on the steaks and press down a sprig of thyme into each steak.
•Heat oil in a pressure cooker and sauté onion and garlic in it.
•Mix in the wine and add the bay leaf.
•Place the steamer basket in the cooker and place the salmon steaks on it.
•Close the pressure cooker and place the pressure regulator on the vent pipe.
•Cook at 15 lbs. pressure for 2 minutes, with the regulator rocking slowly.
•Cool the pressure cooker and remove the salmon steaks and place in a platter.
•Discard the bay leaf and remove the steamer basket.
•Combine the tapioca starch with 2 tbsp. mustard and blend it into the sauce in the cooker.
•Cook until the sauce thickens and then serve with the steaks.

Paleo Pressure Cooker Poached Salmon
(Servings: 4)

INGREDIENTS:

16 oz. salmon fillet with the skin on
4 scallions, trimmed
Zest of 1 lemon
3 black peppercorns
½ tsp. fennel seeds
1 tsp. white wine vinegar
1 bay leaf
½ cup dry white wine
2 cups chicken broth
¼ cup fresh dill
Salt and Pepper

INSTRUCTIONS:

•Season the salmon fillets with salt and pepper.
•Place the fish in a trivet and place the trivet in the pressure cooker.
•Pour the wine, vinegar and broth over the fish and place the rest of the ingredients atop the fish fillets.

•Close the pressure cooker and bring to pressure on high heat.
•Reduce the heat and cook for 4 minutes.
•Cool the pressure cooker and place the salmon on a serving platter.
•Cook the sauce until reduced and pour over the fish.

Paleo Pressure Cooker Shrimps Piquant
(Servings: 4)

INGREDIENTS:

2 tbsp. olive oil
1 ½ lbs. large shrimps, de-shelled
1 cup minced onion
2 tbsp. minced parsley
4 cloves garlic, minced
2 tsp. paprika
¼ cup dry white wine
½ cup clam juice
1 cup tomato sauce
1 tsp. honey
Pinch of saffron
1 tsp. crushed hot red pepper
1 bay leaf
¼ tsp. thyme
Salt, freshly ground pepper to taste

INSTRUCTIONS:

•Heat the olive oil in a pressure cooker and sauté the shrimps in it over high flame for a minute. Transfer the shrimps to a plate.
•Sauté the onions in the oil and add the parsley, garlic, paprika.
•Pour the wine and bring to boil, reducing the wine by half.
•Add the clam juice, saffron, tomato sauce, bay leaf, red pepper, thyme, salt, pepper and honey.
•Close the pressure cooker and bring to pressure.
•At high pressure cook for 4 minutes.
•Release the pressure, open the lid and if required cook additionally to thicken the sauce.
•Add the shrimps back, close the cover and bring to pressure.
•Cook for 2 minutes and then release the pressure.
•Discard the bay leaf prior to serving.

Paleo Pressure Cooker Raspberry Herbed Salmon
(Servings: 6)

INGREDIENTS:

6 salmon steaks (1 inch thick)
1 pint raspberry vinegar
2 tbsp. olive oil
4 leeks, cut into 1/2 inch slices
2 garlic cloves, crushed
2 tbsp. minced fresh parsley
1 cup bottled clam juice
2 tbsp. fresh lemon juice
1 tsp. sherry
1 tsp. salt
1/2 tsp. white pepper
1/3 cup chopped fresh dill
Fresh raspberries, for garnish

INSTRUCTIONS:

•Marinate the steaks in the raspberry vinegar and refrigerate for 3 hours covered.
•Heat oil in a pressure cooker and sauté the garlic, parsley and leeks in it for 2 minutes.
•Pour in the clam juice, sherry and lemon juice and add the pepper, salt and dill, stirring well.
•Transfer the salmon steaks from the marinade to the sauce in the pressure cooker.
•Close the pressure cooker and bring to high pressure.
•Reduce the heat and cook for 3 minutes.
•Release the pressure, using the auto release technique and uncover the cooker.
•Transfer to a serving dish and top with some fresh raspberries.

Paleo Pressure Cooked Calamari
(Servings: 4-6)

INGREDIENTS:

1 ½ lbs. calamari fresh, cleaned well and cut into rounds
1 (14.5 oz.) can of chopped tomatoes
1/2 glass of white wine
1 garlic clove, smashed
1 bunch parsley, chopped
2 anchovies
1 pinch of hot pepper
1 Lemon, juiced
Olive Oil
Salt & pepper

INSTRUCTIONS:

•Add oil, a pinch of hot pepper, garlic and anchovies to the pressure cooker and place on low flame, tossing the ingredients around to flavor the oil.
•Add the calamari and color them lightly.
•Pour in the wine and allow it to slightly evaporate.
•Add the tomatoes and half the chopped parsley.
•Refill the tomato can with water and pour the water into the pressure cooker. Stir the ingredients.
•Close the pressure cooker and bring to high pressure.
•Reduce the heat and cook for 15-20 minutes at high pressure.
•Release the pressure and uncover the cooker.
•Stir in the lemon juice, some olive oil and parsley.

Paleo Pressure Cooker Fish Chowder

INGREDIENTS:

2 frozen blocks skinless, boneless haddock, cut in chunks
4 sweet potatoes, diced
1 small onion, diced
1 can chicken broth
1 can water
1 can coconut milk
Salt & Pepper

INSTRUCTIONS:

•Place all the ingredients, except the salt and pepper in a pressure cooker and cook covered for 8-10 minutes after raising the pressure.
•Release the pressure naturally and then uncover the cooker.
•Season with salt and pepper.
•Divide the mixture into two portions and cook one portion at a time until thickened slightly, stirring frequently

Paleo Pressure Cooker Clam Chowder
(Servings: 4-6)

INGREDIENTS:

2 dozen middle neck clams, rinsed well
1 cup chicken broth
½ cup bacon, diced very small
1 tbsp. olive oil
1 cup yellow onion, chopped very fine
2 garlic cloves, chopped very fine
½ cup celery, chopped very fine
½ cup white wine
1 bay leaf
2 cups sweet potatoes, diced medium
2 tbsp. almond butter
2 tbsp. coconut flour
1½ cups coconut cream
½ cup coconut milk
½ tsp. Tabasco

INSTRUCTIONS:

•Place the clams along with chicken broth in the steamer basket of a pressure cooker.

- Close the pressure cooker and bring to pressure on high heat.
- Reduce the heat from high to low and cook for 4 minutes.
- Release the pressure using cold water and remove the clams and place aside.
- Strain the liquid into a bowl and place aside.
- Clean the pressure cooker and add bacon with some oil on medium flame.
- Add onions after a minute and sauté for 2 minutes.
- Add and stir fry the celery and garlic for 3 minutes.
- Pour in the white wine and cook until reduced by half.
- Pour in the strained clam broth along with the bay leaf and sweet potatoes.
- Close the pressure cooker and bring to pressure on high heat.
- Reduce the heat from high to medium and cook for 4 minutes.
- Release the pressure using cold water, remove lid and place on a medium flame.
- Heat the almond butter in a pan over medium flame and mix in the flour after melted, stirring continuously. Place aside.
- Pour the coconut flour mix into the pressure cooker and blend into the soup.
- Add the coconut cream, coconut milk, tobacco and the clams.
- Season with salt and pepper and allow to heat through.

Paleo Pressure Cooker Steamed Mussels

INGREDIENTS:

2 lbs. Mussels, cleaned and de-bearded
1 White Onion, chopped
1 Small head of Radicchio, cut into thin strips
1 lb. of Baby Spinach
1 clove of Garlic, smashed
½ cup dry white wine
½ cup of water
Olive Oil

INSTRUCTIONS:

•Place the mussels in a steamer basket and keep aside.
•Heat a swirl of olive oil in a pressure cooker and sauté the onions and garlic cloves in it.
•Deglaze the bottom of the pressure cooker using the white wine and then place the steamer basket with the mussels in the pressure cooker.
•Close the pressure cooker and cook for a minute on low pressure.
•Release the pressure naturally.
•Place a layer of spinach and radicchio strips on a serving platter and place the mussels on top of it.
•Serve the broth along with the mussels.

Paleo Pressure Cooked Lobsters

INGREDIENTS:

5 1-lb lobsters
1/2 cup white wine
1 cup water

INSTRUCTIONS:

•Place the lobsters, water and wine in the inner pot and place the inner pot in the power cooker.
•Close the cooker and close the pressure release valve.
•Press the Fish option button and adjust the time to reach 5 minutes.
•After the timer reaches zero, the cooker automatically switches to keep warm.
•Open the pressure release valve.
•After the pressure is released , uncover and remove the lobsters.

Paleo Pressure Cooked King Crabs

INGREDIENTS:

4 lbs. King Crab Legs, break to fit into the cooker
1 cup water
3 lemon wedges

INSTRUCTIONS:

•Place the crab legs and water in the inner pot and place the inner pot in the power cooker.
•Close the cooker and close the pressure release valve.
•Press the Fish option button and adjust the time to reach 3 minutes.
•After the timer reaches zero, the cooker automatically switches to keep warm.
•Open the pressure release valve.
•After the pressure is released, uncover and remove the crab legs.
•Serve with lemon wedges.

Paleo Pressure Cooker Steamed Lobster Tails
(Servings: 4)

INGREDIENTS:

1 cup Water
1-2 lbs. Lobster Tails, chopped into half from top to tail
Ghee, melted
Celtic Sea Salt

INSTRUCTIONS:

•Place the lobster tails, shell side down in a steamer basket and place the steamer basket in the pressure cooker.
•Close the cooker and bring to low pressure over high heat.
•Reduce the heat once the pressure is reached and steam for 3 minutes.
•Release the pressure using the quick release method.
•Using tongs transfer the lobster tails into a serving platter.
•Sprinkle salt over the tails and serve with melted ghee.

Conclusion

Thank you again for downloading this book!

I hope this book was able to help you discover some amazing Pressure Cooker Recipes. The next step is to get cooking!!!

FREE Gift -Healthy Pressure Cooker Recipes

As a "Thank You" for purchasing this book, I want to give you a gift absolutely 100% Free

Go to http://freebookbonus.com/pressure-cooker

Printed in Great Britain
by Amazon